Handmade Jewelry

*How to Make Jewelry for Beginners and Create
Unique Custom Pieces on a Budget*

Table of Contents

Introduction

I want to thank you and congratulate you for downloading the book, "Handmade Jewelry -How to Make Jewelry for Beginners and Create Unique Custom Pieces on a Budget".

This book contains proven steps and strategies that can help you make your own jewelry!

If you take the time to read this book fully and apply the information held within, this book will help you learn and understand the techniques of making your own jewelry.

Are you looking for a new pursuit that will bring out your creative side? Are you passionate about creating beautiful things? Designing a piece of jewelry will give you a very rewarding feeling. If you are looking for a new hobby or pastime that will allow you to explore your creative side, then this might be for you.

Creating jewelry indeed sounds intimidating at first, but like all things, it can be learned. This book is ideal for beginners who want to learn the ropes of making their own jewelry from various materials. You won't just enjoy wearing beautiful pieces, you'll get to enjoy making them too! You can even give your works to friends and family. Once you are more confident, you can even turn this into a profitable business.

Browse through the pages of this book and learn the basics of making beautiful works of art.

Thanks again for downloading this book, I hope you enjoy it!

Chapter 1

Understanding the Basics

There are only a few people who don't appreciate the beauty of jewelry. Pieces of jewelry in their most basic form are beautiful works of art which show the creativity and talent of human beings. We have the ability to appreciate beauty and we go the extra mile to look good. We can create detailed pieces that can help accentuate our natural features. We know how to use our resources to capture the essence of beauty. Jewelry is more than just a form of luxury. It is provides a glimpse of how beautiful the soul of humankind can be. Jewelry is more than an accessory, it can provide meaningful symbolisms that reflect our creativity and resourcefulness.

The art of making jewelry started way, way back. Believe it or not, it was believed that our early ancestors learned how to make jewelry as soon as they learned how to make their own tools. Back then, diamonds, rubies and emeralds were not yet appreciated, so the first jewelry were made from easily-available natural materials. During the ancient times, they probably used animal teeth and bone, carved stone and wood to make different pieces of jewelry. It seems that the earliest kinds of jewelry were actually very functional. For example, they were used to fasten pieces of clothing together. Later on, the jewelry they started to use became more for ornamental purposes, the same way we use jewelry nowadays. It was believed that jewelry helped them connect to the spiritual and mysterious. In a sense, it became a spiritual and religious symbol.

As time progressed, jewelry eventually became a symbol of wealth and status. Gold became the material of choice for expensive jewelry. Various kinds of jewelry like bracelets, necklaces, eating and rings became very popular. If a person wears and displays more gold, he or she is considered more elite. It was considered so valuable that it was even buried with the dead to be considered as adornment in the afterlife.

The seventeenth century was an important time for the history of jewelry making because this is when cutting techniques improved, and also the possibility of worldwide trade of gemstones paved the path for more style designs. The different styles of jewelry became more diverse.

Over the years, more and more developments in jewelry style and jewelry-making appeared. Nowadays, women particularly enjoy wearing jewelry. It usually helps them feel more beautiful and valuable. It can also make them feel more fashionable and trendy.

The jewelry you choose to wear says a lot about yourself. While some like wearing classic styles and expensive jewelry, there are those who like to keep things hip, trendy and unique. Either way, it is safe to say that most women like wearing jewelry that will help compliment their looks.

Unfortunately, buying jewelry, even fancy or costume ones, can be very expensive. If you want to start a collection, one thing that you can do is to learn how to make your own jewelry.

Making your own jewelry can be a ton of fun and it is a good way for you to release your creative juices. Perhaps creating your own jewelry may seem overwhelming at first, but you don't need to be a crafty artist in order to come up with something beautiful. It can take some time to get there, but it is entirely possible to master the skill of making your own jewelry without any strong artistic background. Let's take it one step at a time until you are comfortable with making your own stuff.

Making your own jewelry is a good way to release stress. It is a nice hobby that can help you relax in spite of your daily problems. Learning this skill can also help increase your confidence. Some even progress to selling their own products online. You never know where this hobby is going to take you, so it is a perfectly good idea to try it out.

Naturally, it is not right to expect that you can make jewelry like a professional can. Especially when you are just starting out, you still need to learn a lot of things in order to be able to create something beautiful. Be patient with yourself as you learn the process. As you make more jewelry, improvement will eventually come. In time, you will come up with more beautiful pieces!

Are you interested in learning how to make your own jewelry? Do you think that you h what it takes to come up with your own earrings or bracelets?

Here are some tips which can help you get in the jewelry-making world.

Getting started

1.Learn what you can

Naturally, when you don't know anything, you will likely feel intimidated about starting this new hobby. The only way to get over your fears is to learn what you can about making jewelry. Try to at least understand the basics of technique, terminology and style. There are many online videos, websites and books which can help you get a grasp of what jewelry-making is all about. Increasing your knowledge will help you be more confident about starting a project. Educate yourself so that you'll actually have the courage to plunge into the actual process of designing and coming up with our very own creations.

It would even be better if you can talk to someone who has this hobby. There is nothing like learning from someone who actually knows how to do it. Join online forums or meet up with someone who is interested in jewelry-making. You can even join a class or workshop if you can. It is good to get firsthand advice and stories. You might even find yourself sharing materials with the people you talk to!

2. Try to determine your style

Are you making jewelry for yourself or are you making them for other people? Try to determine what style you want to focus on at first. It should be simple enough for you to accomplish but unique enough to make an impact. Try to make your personality and preferences come out. The point of DIY is to create one-of-a-kind items, so don't just copy what you see. Try to add a personal touch in whatever you do to make your products more unique and more interesting.

You can start with using one particular technique or with using one particular material. This will prevent you from getting overwhelmed by the numerous options that you can do and use for your DIY crafts. Once you are happy with a particular style or technique, you can move on to handling others, but try to put a "stamp" in the items that you do. Make your items unique and interesting, but add something recognizable so that people will easily be able to tell that it is your work.

3. Set your goals

Why do you want t o learn how to make jewelry anyway? Do you want to expand your own collection? Do you want to give them as gifts? Are you thinking of turning this hobby into a business?

Setting goals is important because it will keep you motivated to stick to what you are doing. It will prevent you from giving up when things get too difficult. Make sure that your goals are clear when you are just starting out. Perhaps your goals will eventually change, but it is always good to map out where you want to start and what you want to achieve.

Making your own jewelry is fulfilling because you will be able to create unique and personalized pieces that can be found nowhere else. You don't need to buy accessories that look exactly like what everyone else is wearing. Furthermore, you'll surely appreciate the fulfilling feeling you'll get after completing a certain piece. It is a different kind of accomplishment when you get to wear something that you actually created.

Giving jewelry as gifts is fulfilling as well. You can create items that will really suit the personalities of the receivers of your gifts. Your gifts will surely meaningful because they will be personalized. You can create a piece based on the individual characters of the receivers and they will surely feel special.

Once you are more comfortable with creating jewelry and once you are more confident with your works, you can start selling them to your relatives and friends. You can even go beyond that and sell your works online. There are many entrepreneurs who sell their products through websites. You may also join community bazaars or you can partner up with stores if you wish.

4. Be patient

It can get frustrating when you don't get to create what you imagine. However, you need to be patient with yourself because you are learning a new skill. It won't be easy at first. Don't be afraid to make mistakes. Eventually, you will get the hang of it. Try to understand the steps of what you are doing. Figure out what you are doing wrong and try to correct what you can. Eventually, you will be able to find the fastest and most efficient way to do things.

Don't give up! If you are really passionate about making jewelry then keep on doing it until you get better. Skill comes with time and experience. Eventually, you will be happy and confident with the pieces that you create. You never know where jewelry-making will take you, so as long as you are passionate about it, then keep on doing it.

5. Have fun

It is important for you to enjoy the process of creation! Don't see it as a chore which needs to be completed. Allow this new hobby to bring out your fun-loving side. If you are happy with what you are doing, it will surely come out in your works. You will be able to create more interesting pieces if you are having fun with what you are doing.

Make sure to enjoy the process of creation. If you feel pressured, then change your approach to designing. Of course, jewelry making means hard work too, but at the end of the day, it should make you feel good about yourself. It should make you feel good that you are able to create beautiful things.

Chapter 2

Tools and Supplies

As you start this hobby, you need to keep in mind that you need tools and supplies that will make it much easier for you to get the job done. You don't need to buy everything all at once, but you need to at least have the basics in order to be able to start. You can start buying the basics first and then eventually just wait for all your supplies to accumulate. Think of these tools and supplies as investments. It may seem like it costs a lot at first, but your expenses are surely worth it in the long run. You will still be able to save more if you make your own jewelry than if you buy.

Much of what you can do depends on what materials you have. If you have high-quality materials and a variety of different tools and supplies, you can expect that you will be able to come up with versatile and beautiful pieces that will stand out. It is also more likely for you to stick to the hobby if you have everything you need. Since it is going to be more convenient for you to work, you will be more motivated and committed.

Here are some of the things that you should keep in mind as you try to make your purchases for this new hobby.

1.Choose quality materials

You don't want your necklace to suddenly snap or the decorations of your earrings to suddenly fall off, do you? Then it is best to invest in quality materials that will allow you to create sturdy items. If your materials are weak and if they are cheaply made, then it wouldn't be surprising to see them break. One of the secrets of being able to create quality products is using quality materials.

Quality products are a bit pricier than usual products, but they are absolutely worth it because they will give you good jewelry. Avoid choosing the cheapest options. If the price is too low, then the quality is probably not so good. However, don't think that you need to choose the most expensive option either. Some quality materials are just in the middle-range. You just have to know how to choose well in order to get a good deal.

Don't worry, even if you choose to invest in more expensive materials, it would still cost less than buying ready-made jewelry. So in the end, you will still be able to save money. Don't feel bad about spending on the materials. Go ahead and give yourself a chance to splurge on quality.

2. Get all the right tools

If you are really serious about this hobby, then you should get all the tools that you will need in creating the jewelry. When you have everything you need, it will be much easier for you to construct the items that you want to create. When it is convenient for you to make your jewelry, it is more likely that you will stick to the hobby.

Get all the tools that will make jewelry-making easier for you. Invest in the right scissors and pliers. Scout craft stores in your area and purchase the items which you think will make it easier for you to make your jewelry. Remember that you will be using these tools for a long time so do your research to ensure that you will get the best value for your money.

You might also want to invest in a case or toolbox that will help you organize all your tools and supplies. Make storage convenient so that you won't need to search for your tools every time you want to make something.

3. Use a bead board

There are some tools and equipment which are really meant to make jewelry-making easier for you. Try to find out what these tools are and invest in them. It will make the process of jewelry-making much easier and you can use your energy to focus on creating beautiful designs.

A bead board is something that can really help you with the designs of your project. You can easily just lay out your beads and change up the designs until you are satisfied. You don't even need to use thread! You can also avoid the hassle of having to redo everything if you are not satisfied with the designs. A bead board will allow you to see how your piece would look once it's finished, and it will allow you to conveniently change the beads without any trouble. In addition to this, bead boards usually have a plastic snap-on. This will make your project portable so you don't have to worry about your half-finished projects.

4. Use quality jump rings

Many jewelry makers understand the importance of jump rings. Jump rings have many uses and they can make jewelry construction so much easier for you. Generally speaking, jump rings are used to connect jewelry parts such as clasps, clamps and charms. However, they have many other uses. You can also use jump rings to remedy jewelry items that are broken. You can use these to fill gaps in your projects. You can even use them to decorate your creations! Jump rings are essential in any jewelry maker's toolbox.

Choose jump rings that are sturdy, and if you can, try to pick ones that won't tarnish. Jump rings are also available in various sizes so feel free to buy different kinds. They are typically available in packs of 100, but it is likely that you'll use them all anyway. Just store everything in an organizer or supplies box. No matter how many you have, you will eventually find a use for them anyway.

5. Make sure to use high-quality bead-thread

It will be a major problem if the thread you use for your beaded projects are weak and fragile. It can get embarrassing if your jewelry snaps in two and causes beads to scatter. One way to proven this is to make sure that you use high-quality bead-thread that won't break easily. For your convenience, try to pick fiber with extra-strength for all your stringing projects.

FireLine is a brand that is recommended by a lot of expert jewelry-makers. It is ideal for beginners because it is easy to use and it doesn't tangle easily. It is ideal for off-loom weaving and stringing projects involving small pearls and gemstone beads.

You can easily purchase FireLine in a lot of various craft stores. Keep in mind that you need to you need to purchase the right size that will suit your needs perfectly. FireLine threads are sized according to strength. For example, if you buy a size ten thread, it means that it would take ten pounds to break this particular thread. Other sizes are available as well.

6. Use crimping pliers

Crimping pliers is a tool that should be used when crimping beads. Crimping pliers are useful because they can give your works a more polished look. Don't try to use ordinary pliers because they just don't look the same. Crimping pliers may seem complicated to use for beginners but once you get the hang of it, you will see how convenient it is to use crimping pliers.

7. Use anything around you!

A huge part of creation is knowing how to maximize the materials that you have at your disposal. You need to learn how to be resourceful if you want your works to be unique. Look around you. What are the things that you can use to create beautiful pieces? Buttons? Bottle caps? Coins?

Try to be resourceful. Some of the most unique items are actually from recycled materials and random household items. Since the eco-movement is now very popular, you can help transform trash into something more useful and much more beautiful. This can even be the defining factor of all your works! There would be a lot of consumers who would appreciate your works even more if they see that you have an advocacy.

Chapter 3

Principles of Design

One of the nicest things about jewelry design is that it can really help bring out your creative side. It is an avenue for you to be artistic. Many hobbyists find it relaxing to make unique jewelry on their free time because it allows them to express themselves. It allows them to take a break from their busy and hectic lives, even just for a while.

One thing that will really help you understand how to make jewelry is to take apart your favorite piece of accessory and try to re-assemble it. What would you do differently? Do you think that you can do better than this? What design principles would you apply?

It would also help if you keep yourself updated with the history and development of jewelry design. And of course, you should also try to keep up with the latest trends. Study how jewelry design developed over the decades. There are a lot of magazines and websites which you can learn from. These can serve as your inspiration as you come up with something of your own.

When you are creating your jewelry, keep in mind that the finished products may be different from how you envision them to be. So it is important to be flexible and open. Be ready to make changes in case your piece is different from what you want. Don't feel bad. This is all part of the creation process. Don't get frustrated or disappointed with yourself. Hopefully, with just a few tweaks in your design, you'll be able to come up with something that you'll be happy with.

When designing anything, you can't just put everything in and expect that it would come out beautifully. It is possible to add too much and end up over designing your work. Some elements might look out of place so make sure to plan out everything first. Over designed works can be a pain in the eyes.

Keep in mind that in the design process, mistakes are most welcome. In fact, some of the most cherished designs resulted from mistakes. You might be surprised by how nice your mistakes can possibly turn out to be. So don't be afraid to make mistakes. No jewelry maker has made all his or her works perfect.

The art of jewelry-making is very visual, so it is important to determine what visual message you are sending through your works. Even in jewelry-making, you can apply the simple principles of design that can help you come up with beautiful jewelry pieces.

Here are the basic design principles which you can apply in making your own jewelry.

1.Balance

Balance refers to the equal distribution of weight, colors, materials and other design elements which make up your piece. Symmetry is an important principle of beauty. It is important for you piece to have a sense of balance. For example, if one side of your necklace has a lot of small elements, you can balance it out by putting a large piece of decor on the other side. This will make the piece appear more balanced. Keep in mind that weight is not the only factor which will affect the symmetry of your work. Visual balance is important too. This means that your work should appear balanced when it comes to color, texture and material.

Keep in mind that asymmetrical balance and radial balance works well too. You just have to play with the concepts to figure out if this will work. Asymmetrical balance means informal balance where you purposely make one side appear heavier than the other. Generally speaking, it appears more casual and less planned but it is actually the result of creative thinking and artistic presentation of the elements you want to present. Radial balance is where the elements "radiate" from one central point. Items with radial balance will usually lead your eyes to once focal point in the center of the piece.

2. Emphasis

Emphasis can be somewhat understood as dominance. It is the part of the jewelry piece which will really catch the attention of whoever will look at it. Generally speaking, it is good to have only one focal point for your work because it might appear messy if there are too many focal points. Everything will appear more harmonious if there is only one focus. All the tiny details should highlight the point of emphasis in the jewelry.

3. Movement

A good piece of jewelry will feel like it has a flowing design. A piece with good movement should feel like there are no breaks when you look at it. The way your eyes would move through the piece would determine if your creation has good movement. It should feel smooth and harmonious. You can achieve this by paying attention to the tiny details that you include in what you do. A lot of designers achieve this through repetition and rhythm.

4. Proportion

Proportion can be more easily understood as the relationship of a certain area to another area or to the whole piece. Usually, proportion will only be appreciated if a piece lacks it. It is easy to see if something is out of proportion. It would look unbalanced and mismatched. In other words, it won't look good.

5. Contrast

Contrast means trying to make two opposing elements work. It is interesting to use contrast because it uses things that are seemingly in conflict but somehow still creates harmony. Pieces of jewelry that has an element of contrast are ideal for those who want to create wild, interesting, and bold pieces. If you want to make a statement, then this is something for you. Make jewelry with contrasting designs to make your work stand out. Try using colors in the opposing ends of the color wheel or using different directions of design. Using contrast in the right way will give your pieces a harmonious overall look.

6. Unity

Every single detail that you put into your work should contribute something to the whole picture. All the elements should appear like they belong together. No matter how wild a detail may be, it should still fit in. You are trying to create a whole, so every single element that you include should appear unified with the rest.

One thing you can do to ensure that your jewelry would appear to have a unified design is to create a theme for your work. Make sure that all the elements you add would contribute something to the theme. If it doesn't fit, then it would be best to just remove it.

A skilled artist will be able to create a unified design even if there are seemingly out-of-this-world elements. However, this would require years of experience and a very good eye. Since you are just starting out, you can do trial-and-error until you find out what works.

7. Harmony

Harmony is how the details of your work relate to one another. This can be easily achieved by making sure that there is something similar in whatever you add in your work. Sometimes it's about the color, sometimes it's about the material, sometimes it's about the texture. The important thing is that there is something similar that connects the elements together. You will know that a piece is harmonious when you look at it and everything just feels right.

Chapter 4

Making Your Own Jewelry

Here are simple guidelines which can help you in your first project. Keep in mind that these are just suggestions and you have the option to change or adjust the pieces as you see fit.

1. Casual Bracelet

A casual bracelet is easy to make and it is ideal for those who want something unique and personalized to complement their outfits. Since the materials used for casual bracelets are not so expensive, you can also give the as gifts. This casual bracelet is so easy, you can even ask your kids to make it.

Start by preparing your materials. For this project, you need old buttons of different kinds and sizes. You can either look for old buttons you have at home or buy new buttons of different kinds. The more varied and colorful your buttons are, the better your necklace would look. Regular, two-hole buttons are perfect for this project. You will also need a fishing line or nylon to string together the buttons you've prepared.

Gauge the length of string that you would need for the bracelet. Make sure to give it allowance because you'll need to secure both ends of the bracelet. Start by inserting the fishing line up through one whole and down through the other. Continue doing this again and again until you reach the length you desire. Try to make sure that your design has a pattern. Apply the principles of design as you choose what buttons to include in your bracelet.

Make sure that the ends of the bracelet are secure. You can then add the clasp of your choice. Check and double-check everything to ensure that the clasps won't fall off. Try to ensure that the bracelet itself is sturdy as well. This is a great addition to everyday outfits! It would add charm, color and quirkiness to whatever you are planning to wear.

2. Bottle cap earrings

For another casual piece of jewelry, you can try making unique bottle cap earrings that will display your favorite contemporary beverages. If you have contemporary bottle caps, you can use those too. They are hip, attractive and very easy to do.

Start by preparing the materials you need. Have 2 matching bottle caps, 2 head pins, 2 ear wires and beads for design. As tools you'll need a small hammer, jewelry pliers and round-nose jewelry pliers. If you don't have these tools yet, try to be resourceful. Modify what you have with you in order to get the work done.

Don't work on a glass table. One of the first things that you should do is to make sure that the surface that you're working on is protected. Start by punching holes on the bottle caps. You can use this using a screwdriver, nail or AWL. Hammer the end of the screwdriver, nail or awl to the position where you want the hole to be. Be careful because the hammer could very easily hurt you.

Slip the head pin in the hole. Make sure that the pin is secure. The head of the pin should be inside the cap. You can then add the beads of your choice to the head pin. In effect, there would be something dangling that would make the earrings more attractive and colorful. Choose beads that match the color of your bottle cap. Also, make sure that you secure both ends of your pin so that the beads on your earrings won't fall off. You have the option to add as many holes as you can to add more beads or even a dangling chain. Play around with your materials and explore what you can do to give your work a unique and creative look.

Attach the ear wires and try on your earrings! Now you have a beautiful accessory and a nice conversation piece that will surely catch the eye of people around you.

3. Washer necklace

In this project, you can use washers to create a beautiful neck piece that will really catch the attention of people around you. Washers can be easily bought in hardware stores. By using your creativity, washers can be transformed into a beautiful necklace.

Start by preparing the materials you need. You'll need pliers, about ten washers or so (depending on how big and attractive you want your necklace to be); about twelve jump rings, a chain, and a bottle of nail polish in your favorite color. Lay down all your materials and get ready to work.

Start by painting one side of the washers and let dry. If you want, you can use different colors in painting the washers. You can even design them. It all depends on your personal style. Next, connect the washer to one another using the jump rings. You can form any shape you want. You can keep it simple or you can make it a bit more interesting. Currently, the trend is to wear V-shaped necklaces so you might want to consider making something like that. Play around with the washers until you come up with something which you think you will like.

Once you are happy with the way your washers are arranged, the next thing you can do is to attach the chain. Figure out which are the two ends of your washer arrangement. Connect each end of to the end of the chain to form the necklace. Adjust the length as needed.

Check the washers if any of them has chipped or cracked polish. Re-paint them and let dry. If you want, you can top with a clear nail polish to give your painted washers additional protection.

Conclusion

Thank you again for downloading this book!

I hope this book was able to help you to understand the basic concepts of jewelry making.

The next step is to head to the craft store and buy the materials you'll need.

Making jewelry can be such a fun and exciting experience. Though it can be quite challenging at first, it can be very fulfilling once you understand the basics. Some people find it very relaxing to explore designs. Making jewelry is a good way to release stress, especially if you want to do something light and relaxing.

Try to understand the basic principles of design as you do your work. They can be very helpful in guiding you through the process of creation. However, don't forget to have fun! Make sure that you add unique and personalized touches that will make your works interesting.

Don't be afraid of making mistakes! Just enjoy the creative process and learn what you can in every project. With time and experience, you will get better and better at this.

Finally, if you enjoyed this book, please take the time to share your thoughts and post a review on Amazon. It'd be greatly appreciated!

Thank you and good luck!

Bonus Chapter: Making Bracelets and Necklaces

Beautifully made necklaces and bracelets bring out ones beauty and personality. By making your own necklaces and bracelets, you will be able to express yourself to the world loudly and creatively. They are also a good way of showing your love and appreciation to the people you care about. No expensive gift can beat a handmade necklace or bracelet made with time, effort, and love. The following bracelet and necklace projects will help you make your own first ever handmade jewelry. In mastering these, you can be more creative and add more of "you" into your work.

Project # 1: The Rainbow Strip (String and Bead Necklace)

You will need the following: any stringing medium of your choice, glass or plastic beads of any size of your choice (red, orange, yellow, green, blue, indigo, and violet), blue seed beads, colorless nail polish, ruler and scissors.

First, cut the stringing medium according to your preferred length plus at least 6 inches more (for ease in tying down the stringing medium).

Second, string the beads through and follow the color pattern of rainbows. In between each bead, insert a seed bead. So, you have to string a red bead first, then a seed bead, followed by an orange bead, and so on.

Third, once your preferred length of stringing medium is filled by the beads, draw the opposite ends together and tie a basic square knot.

Finally, brush a little amount of colorless nail polish on the knot to seal it and prevent it from unraveling. Now you have your own rainbow necklace.

Project #2: Crystals in the Night (Wire and Bead Necklace)

You will need the following: round Swarovski crystals (8mm; any color), bead caps (2 for bead), chain nose pliers, jump rings, 20 gauge jewelry wires (silver), ruler, round nose pliers, and flush cutters.

First, make a bead unit (made up of a bead, two bead caps, and a short wire). To make a bead unit, cut up a piece of short wire 1.25 inches in length. Make a loop on one end of this wire, but do not close it completely. On the other end, string in a bead cap, then a bead, and followed by another bead cap. Secure the unit by making another loop at the end (also not completely closed). Make as many bead units as necessary.

Second, connect each bead unit to form your necklace. To do this, just hook one incompletely looped end of a bead unit and another unit. Using round nose pliers, close the loops completely.

Third, if the necklace has reached your desired length, set it aside and make your own hook and catch.

Lastly, attach one end with the hook and the other with the catch. Now you have your own Crystals in the Night necklace.

Project #3: Chain of Hearts (Wire Bracelet)

You will need the following: 18 gauge jewelry wire (gold), jump rings (silver), normal string or yarn, ruler, flush cutter, and round nose pliers.

First, prepare a normal string or yarn with the same length that you want your bracelet to be. This is going to be the basis of how many hearts and jump rings you will use.

Second, cut a few wire pieces of that are 1.5 inches in length.

Third, with the wire held horizontally in front of you, clip the tip of the pliers a few centimeters from one end of the short wire and curl inwards. Do this to the other end of the wire.

Fourth, clip the tip of the pliers on the center of the wire and use your fingers to push each curled end towards each other. Make sure that they actually touch. This will be the wire hearts. Make more of them as you deem fit.

Fifth, connect the hearts with a jump ring between each heart. You can use one or two jump rings if you want. Make sure that each end of the necklace ends in one jump ring.

Sixth, if the chain has reached your desired length, set it aside and make your own hook and catch (as what you have learned in the previous chapter).

Finally, attach one end with the hook and the other with the catch. Now you have your own Chain of Hearts.

Project #4: Green is Love (Multi-strand Bead Bracelet)

You will need the following: stringing medium of your choice, normal string or yarn, 5 kinds of beads of your choice (can be of different sizes; should be green but of different shade for each kind), 18 gauge jewelry wire (silver), 2 eye pins, 2 jump rings, and 2 bead cones.

First, prepare a normal string or yarn with the same length that you want your bracelet to be. This is going to be the basis of how long your bracelet should be.

Second, cut up pieces of your stringing medium of the same length as the yarn or string, plus a few inches.

Third, get a jump ring and attach on it one end of each cut up stringing medium using crimp beads.

Fourth, string on the beads onto each stringing medium, then attach and secure the other ends on another jump ring using crimp beads.

Fifth, attach an eye pin on each jump ring. Take the bead cones and inert them through the other end of the eye pin. If the hole on the bead cone is larger, string one small round bead before and after beading cone. Make a wrapped loop using the extra part of the eye pins.

Sixth, make your own hook and catch. And finally, attach one end with the hook and the other with the catch. Now you have your own multi-strand Green is Love bracelet.